THIS

Book

BELONGS TO:

....

....

Coloring with Christ

Copyright © 2023

All rights reserved.

No parts of the publication may be reproduced, distributed, or transmitted in any form or by any means including photocopying, recording, or other electronic or mechanical methods without prior written permission from the publisher.

Hello!

Thank you for purchasing our Devotional Coloring Book to accompany you on your journey of faith and creativity. May your experience be joyful, transformative, and above all, deeply meaningful.

Coloring has a remarkable way of soothing the soul and focusing the mind, allowing you to connect with the sacred text on a personal level. Whether you're an artist at heart or simply seeking a relaxing way to meditate on scripture, this coloring book is designed to accompany you on your spiritual journey. May you find a source of inspiration, reflection, and a reminder of the love that flows through the pages of the Bible.

I would very much appreciate if you could take a moment to leave a review on Amazon. Please use the QR code to take you directly to the review page.

Thank you so much!

Welcome!

We are excited to extend a warm and heartfelt welcome to you as you embark on a creative and spiritual journey through our Bible Devotional Coloring Book. This book has been created to bring you a unique and enriching experience that combines the joy of coloring with the depth of devotional reflections.

Alongside each illustration, you will find carefully selected verses that encourage contemplation about faith, hope, and love. We encourage you to take your time with each page, letting the words and colors intertwine as you delve deeper into the messages of grace, redemption, and eternal truth.

Take a look at our other journals!

A Verse Mapping Journal & a Sermon Notes Journal!

Available on Amazon!

Pray without ceasing.
1 Thessalonians 5:17

REFLECTIONS:
_____
_____
_____
_____
_____

Rejoice always.

1 Thessalonians 5:16

REFLECTIONS:

_____
_____
_____
_____
_____
_____

Do everything in love.
1 Corinthians 16:14

REFLECTIONS:

_____
_____
_____
_____
_____
_____

Casting all your anxieties on him, because he cares for you.

1 Peter 5:7

REFLECTIONS:

_____
_____
_____
_____
_____
_____

For nothing will be impossible for God.
Luke 1:37

REFLECTIONS:

_____
_____
_____
_____
_____
_____

We love because he first loved us.

1 John 4:19

REFLECTIONS:
_____
_____
_____
_____
_____
_____

Set your mind on things above, not on earthly things.
Colossians 3:2

REFLECTIONS:
_____
_____
_____
_____
_____

When I am afraid, I put my trust in you.

Psalm 56:3

REFLECTIONS:

_____
_____
_____
_____
_____
_____

Reject every kind of evil.

1 Thessalonians 5:22

REFLECTIONS:
_____
_____
_____
_____
_____

Let the word of Christ dwell in you richly.

Colossians 3:16

REFLECTIONS:

_____
_____
_____
_____
_____
_____

He strengthens those who are weak and tired.

Isaiah 40:29

REFLECTIONS:

_____
_____
_____
_____
_____
_____

For everyone has his own burden to bear.

Galatians 6:5

REFLECTIONS:
_____
_____
_____
_____
_____
_____

They are new every morning; great is your faithfulness.

Lamentations 3:23

REFLECTIONS:

_____
_____
_____
_____
_____

For all have sinned and fall short of the glory of God.

Romans 3:23

REFLECTIONS:
_____
_____
_____
_____
_____
_____

I can do all this through him who gives me strength.

Philippians 4:13

REFLECTIONS:

_____
_____
_____
_____
_____
_____

Jesus Christ is the same yesterday, today and forever.

Hebrews 13:8

REFLECTIONS:

_____
_____
_____
_____
_____

Whoever does not love does not know God, because God is love.

1 John 4:8

REFLECTIONS:
_____
_____
_____
_____
_____
_____

Grace be with you all.

Hebrews 13:25

REFLECTIONS:

_____
_____
_____
_____
_____

What time I am afraid, I will trust in You.
Psalm 56:3

REFLECTIONS:
_____
_____
_____
_____
_____

Every good gift and every perfect gift is from above.

James 1:17

REFLECTIONS:
_____
_____
_____
_____
_____
_____

Trust in the Lord with all your heart.
Proverbs 3:5

REFLECTIONS:
_____
_____
_____
_____
_____

Love is patient, love is kind. It does not envy, it does not boast, it is not proud.

1 Corinthians 13:4

REFLECTIONS:

_____
_____
_____
_____
_____

For our God is a consuming fire.
Hebrews 12:29

REFLECTIONS:
___
___
___
___
___
___

The Lord bless you and keep you.
Numbers 6:24

REFLECTIONS:
_____
_____
_____
_____
_____
_____

For my yoke is easy and my burden is light.
Matthew 11:30

REFLECTIONS:

_____
_____
_____
_____
_____
_____

Be merciful, just as your Father is merciful.

Luke 6:36

REFLECTIONS:
_____
_____
_____
_____
_____

For many are invited, but few are chosen.
Matthew 22:14

REFLECTIONS:
_____
_____
_____
_____
_____
_____

I love you, Lord, my strength.

Psalm 18:1

REFLECTIONS:

_____
_____
_____
_____
_____
_____

For we walk by faith, not by sight.
2 Corinthians 5:7

REFLECTIONS:
___
___
___
___
___
___

For everything there is a season, and a time for every matter under heaven.

Ecclesiastes 3:1

REFLECTIONS:
_____
_____
_____
_____
_____
_____

You are the light of the world.
Matthew 5:14

REFLECTIONS:

_____
_____
_____
_____
_____

The Lord is my shepherd, I lack nothing.

Psalm 23:1

REFLECTIONS:

_____
_____
_____
_____
_____

For we walk by faith, not by sight.
2 Corinthians 5:7

REFLECTIONS:
_____
_____
_____
_____
_____

Love must be sincere. Hate what is evil; cling to what is good.

Romans 12:9

REFLECTIONS:

_____
_____
_____
_____
_____

Do not judge, or you too will be judged.
Matthew 7:1

REFLECTIONS:

_____
_____
_____
_____
_____
_____

Be joyful in hope, patient in affliction, faithful in prayer.
Romans 12:12

REFLECTIONS:
_____
_____
_____
_____
_____
_____

Look to the Lord and his strength

1 Chronicles 16:11

REFLECTIONS:
_____
_____
_____
_____
_____

This is the day that the Lord has made; let us rejoice and be glad in it.

Psalm 118:24

REFLECTIONS:

_____
_____
_____
_____
_____
_____

Seek the LORD and his strength; seek his presence continually

1 Chronicles 16:11

REFLECTIONS:

_____
_____
_____
_____
_____
_____

Indeed, "everyone who calls on the name of the Lord will be saved."

Romans 10:13

REFLECTIONS:

_____
_____
_____
_____
_____
_____

In you, Lord my God, I put my trust.
Psalms 25:1

REFLECTIONS:

_____
_____
_____
_____
_____

Do everything without grumbling or arguing.
Philippians 2:14

REFLECTIONS:

_____
_____
_____
_____
_____

Be strong and take heart, all you who hope in the LORD.
Psalm 31:24

REFLECTIONS:

_____
_____
_____
_____
_____

Printed in Great Britain
by Amazon